ETIQUETTE FOR ALL,

OR

Rules of Conduct

FOR EVERY CIRCUMSTANCE IN LIFE:

WITH THE LAWS, RULES, PRECEPTS, AND PRACTICES OF

GOOD SOCIETY.

GLASGOW:

GEORGE WATSON, 58 INGRAM STREET,

1861.

Etiquette for All.

"The manners which one neglects as trifles, are often, precisely that by which men decide on you favourably or the reverse."—BULWER.

GLASGOW :

PRINTED BY GEORGE WATSON, INGRAM STREET.

ETIQUETTE FOR ALL.

Etiquette may be defined as the due observance of a polite and refined manner in our social intercourse. It is the word used to designate the rules and ceremonies recognised and exacted by civilized society, and the knowledge and practice of these, constitute Politeness or Good-breeding. There are various kinds of Etiquette, such as that pertaining to the court of the Sovereign, the Church, the Courts of Law, and the other professions: but in choosing the title of this little Manual, our purpose in its compilation must be understood as restricted to a recapitulation of those rules, precepts, and practices acknowledged by all ranks when brought together by the ordinary exigencies of social life. When we speak of the Etiquette to be observed on any particular occasion, we simply mean the usual and most polite manner in which we can best discharge the duties devolving upon us for the time being. There are few amongst us who have not at times been in the painful situation of doubt and uncertainty regarding the method of procedure in some particular circumstances either public or private. It is our object in this Manual to lay before our readers some of those established rules which obtain in the best circles, and which have been collected and rendered applicable to the present state of society.

Some captious critics may question the necessity of such books as this, and sneer at the seeming shams which people practice in society. Yet all of us must admit that Fashion is omnipotent with the generality of mankind, and that he who would mix with his kind with pleasure to himself and those whose society he seeks, must own her sway and submit to her laws. The philosophic observer is well aware of many absurdities in Fashion and Etiquette that have long survived the natural necessity which called them into existence. The Sage of Chelsea has wisely illustrated this fact by his story of Jean Paul's gentle shepherd, in whose flock a leading ram seeking fresher pasture in a neighbouring field, leaped the barrier to gain his end, and being followed by the rest of the sheep, who tore their wool in following the example, the good man removed the fence so that they might walk through without impediment.—Still the flock kept leaping in the air as if the barrier had still been there.　And so it is with Fashion. Some leading ram, perhaps with toothache in his sinister jaw, to save the twinge, took his soup from the side of his spoon, which all the other guests observing, must needs assume that it was proper for them to do so too. When the Empress Eugenie first invented Crinoline, there was a natural necessity for it, and it was modest in her to do so.　The fashion has been universally adopted, and still it spreads, though the original cause of its use has long since disappeared.　And thus it will be to the end of the chapter.　Let any one, therefore, instead of fretting and making himself miserable by railing at what he cannot mend (and probably does not under-stand), endeavour to discern the difference between frivolous trifling and true politeness, which latter is always founded on the natural instinct and the clear perceptions of a healthy intellect.

IMPORTANCE OF GOOD BEHAVIOUR.

The importance of good behaviour, or in other words, true politeness, can hardly be over-estimated : it gives so much grace and elegance to the most simple sayings and actions. A man's fortune is frequently for ever decided by his first address.—If it be pleasing, people are hurried involuntarily into a persuasion that he has a merit which possibly he has not: as, on the other hand, if it be ungraceful, they are immediately prejudiced against him, and unwilling to allow him the merit which, it may be, he has. The carriage of a gentleman should be genteel, and his motions graceful. He should be particularly careful of his manner and address when he presents himself in company. Let them be respectful without meanness, easy without too much familiarity, genteel without affectation, and insinuating without any seeming act or design. Men, as well as women, are much oftener led by their hearts than by their understandings. The way to the heart is through the senses; please their eyes and their ears, and the work is half done. And since a person with refined manners is always a person who pleases well in good society, let us say a few words upon the importance of the art of pleasing, and how it may be acquired. Let us in the very outset state that the desire of pleasing is at least half the art of doing it; the rest depends solely on the manner which attention, observation, and frequenting good company will teach. Those who are careless or indifferent whether they please or not, will never please. The art is a very necessary one to possess, but a difficult one to acquire. To do as one would be done by, is the surest method of pleasing. Observe carefully what pleases us in others, and probably the same things in us will please others. If we are pleased with the complaisance, and attentions of others to our humours, our tastes, or our weaknesses, the same complaisance and attention on our part to theirs, will equally please them. Let us be serious, gay, or even trifling, as we find the present humour of the company: this is an attention due from every individual to the majority. The art of pleasing cannot be reduced to a receipt; if it could, that receipt would be worth purchasing at any price. Good sense and good nature are the principal ingredients; and our own observation, and the good advice of others, must give the right colour and taste to it.

The graces of the person, the countenance, and the way of speaking, are essential things: and the very same thing said by a genteel person, in an engaging way, and gracefully and distinctly spoken, would please those whom it would shock, if muttered out by an awkward figure with a sullen serious countenance. The poets represent Venus as attended by the Three Graces, to intimate that even beauty will not do without them. Minerva ought to have three also: for without them, learning has few attractions.

If we examine ourselves seriously, why particular people please and engage us more than others of equal merit, we shall always find that it is because the former have the graces and the latter not. Many a woman with an exact shape and a symmetrical assemblage of beautiful features, pleases nobody; while another, with very moderate shape and features has charmed everybody. Among men, how often has the most solid merit been neglected, unwelcome, or even rejected from the want of these graces of manner; while flimsy parts, little knowledge, and less merit has been received, cherished, and admired.

GOOD-BREEDING.

Good-breeding has been very justly defined to be "the result of good sense, some good-nature, and a little self-denial for the sake of others, and with a view to obtain the same indulgence from them." Good-breeding alone can prepossess people in our favour at first sight: more time being necessary to discover greater talents. Good-breeding does not, however, consist in low bows, and formal ceremony, but in an easy, civil, and respectful behaviour.

Indeed, good-sense, in many cases, must determine good-breeding: for what would be civil at one time, and to one person, would be rude at another time, and to another person. There are, however, some general rules of good-breeding. For instance, to answer only yes, or no, to any person, without adding, Sir, Madam (as the case may be), is always rude; and it is equally so not to give proper attention and a civil answer when spoken to. Such behaviour convinces the person who is speaking to us, that we despise him, and do not think him worthy of our attention, or an answer.

A well-bred person will take care to answer with complaisance when he is spoken to; will place himself at the lower end of the table, unless bid to go higher; will not eat awkwardly, nor sit when others stand; and he will do all this with an air of complaisance, and not with a grave ill-natured look, as if he did it unwillingly. There is nothing more difficult to attain, or so necessary to possess as perfect good-breeding; which is equally inconsistent with a stiff formality, an impertinent forwardness, and an awkward bashfulness. A little ceremony is sometimes necessary, a certain degree of firmness is absolutely so, and an awkward modesty is extremely unbecoming.

Virtue and learning, like gold, have their intrinsic value; but if they are not polished, they certainly lose a great deal of their lustre; and even polished brass will pass upon more people than rough gold. Very few, scarcely any, are awanting in the respect which they should show to those whom they acknowledge to be infinitely their superiors. The man of fashion and of the world expresses it in its fullest extent, but naturally, easily, and without concern; whereas a man, who is not used to keep good company, expresses it awkwardly: one sees that he is not used to it, and that it costs him a great deal. Even the worst-bred man living will not be guilty of lolling, whistling, scratching his head, and such like indecencies, in company that he respected. In such companies, therefore, the only point to be attended to is, to show that respect, which everybody means to show, in an easy, unembarrassed and graceful manner.

In mixed companies, whoever is admitted to make part of them, is, for the time being at least, supposed to be upon a footing of equality with the rest; and consequently every one claims, and very justly, every mark of civility and good-breeding. Ease is allowed, but carelessness and negligence are strictly forbidden. If a man accosts you, and talks to you ever so frivolously, it is worse than rudeness—it is brutality to show him, by a manifest inattention to what he says, that you think him a fool or a block-head, and not worth hearing. It is much more with regard to women, who, of whatever rank they are, are entitled, in consideration of their sex, not only to an attentive, but an officious good-breeding from men. Their little wants, likes, dislikes, preferences, antipathies, fancies, whims, and even impertinences, must be officiously attended to, flattered, and, if possible, guessed at and anticipated by a well-bred man. You must never usurp to yourself those conveniences which are of common right, such as the best places, the best dishes, &c., but on the contrary, always decline them yourself, and offer them to others, who, in their turn, who will offer them to you; so that, upon the whole, you will enjoy your share of common right.

The third sort of good-breeding is local, and is variously modified, in not only different countries, but in different towns of the same country. A man of sense carefully attends to the local manners of the respective places where he is, and takes for his models those persons whom he observes to be at the head of the fashion. He watches how they address themselves to their superiors, how they accost their equals, and how they treat their inferiors, and lets none of those little niceties escape him, which are to good-breeding what the last delicate and masterly touches are to a good picture, and which the vulgar have no notion of, but by which good judges distinguish the master. He attends even to their air, dress and motions, and imitates them liberally not servilely: he copies, but does not mimic. These personal graces are of very great consequence. They anticipate the sentiments, before merit can engage the understanding. In short, as it is necessary to possess learning, honour, and virtue, to gain the esteem and admiration of mankind, so politeness and good-breeding are equally necessary to render us agreeable in conversation and common life.

Great talents are above the generality of the world, who neither possess them themselves, nor are competent judges of them in others. But all are judges of the lesser talents, such as civility, affability, and an agreeable address and manner, because they feel the good effects of them, as making society easy and agreeable. Be assured that the profoundest learning, without good-breeding, is unwelcome and tiresome pedantry; that a man who is not perfectly well-bred, is unfit for good company, and unwelcome in it; and that a man who is not well-bred at all is just as unfit for business as for company. Observe then, carefully, the behaviour and manners of those who are distinguished for their good-breeding. Imitate, nay endeavour to excel, that you may at last reach them; and be convinced that good-breeding is, to all worldly qualifications, what charity is to all christian virtues. Observe how it adorns merit, and how often it covers the want of it.

DIGNITY OF MANNERS.

A certain dignity of manners is absolutely necessary to make even the most valuable character either respected or respectable in the world. Practical joking, romping, frequent and loud fits of laughter, waggery, and indiscriminate familiarity, will sink both merit and knowledge into a degree of contempt. They compose at most a merry fellow, and a merry fellow was never yet a respectable man. Indiscriminate familiarity either offends your superiors, or else dubs you their dependant. It gives your inferiors just, but troublesome and improper claims of equality. A joker is near akin to the baboon, and neither of them is the least related to wit. Whoever is admitted or sought for in company, upon any other account than that of his merit and manners, is never respected there, but only made use of. We will have such a one, for he sings prettily; we will invite such a one to a ball, for he dances well; we will have such a one at supper, for he is always joking and laughing; we will ask another because he is a capital fellow for a party. These are all vile distinctions and mortifying preferences, and exclude all ideas of esteem and regard. Whoever is *had* (as it is called) in company, for the sake of any one thing singly, is singly that thing, and will never be considered in any other light, and consequently never respected, let his merits be what they may.

Dignity of manners is not only as different from pride, as true courage is from blustering, or true wit from joking, but it is absolutely inconsistent with it; for nothing vilifies and degrades more than pride. The pretensions of the proud man are oftener treated with sneers and contempt than with indignation; as we offer ridiculously too little to a tradesman, who asks ridiculously too much for his goods; but we do not haggle with one who only asks a just and reasonable price.

Abject flattery and indiscriminate assent degrade, as much as indiscriminate contradiction and noisy debate disgust. But a modest assertion of one's own opinion, and a complaisant acquiescence to other people's, preserve dignity. Vulgar, low expressions, awkward motions and address, vilify, as they imply either a very low turn of mind, or low education and low company. Frivolous curiosity about trifles, and a laborious attention to little objects, which neither deserve nor require a moment's thought, lower a man. From these it is inferred, and not unjustly, that the person who is devoted to them, is incapable of greater matters. Cardinal de Retz very sagaciously marked out Cardinal Chigi for a little mind, from the moment that he told him he had written three years with the same pen, and that it was an excellent one still.

A certain degree of exterior seriousness in looks and motions, gives dignity, without excluding wit and decent cheerfulness, which are always serious in themselves. A constant smirk upon the face, and a whiffling activity of the body, are strong indications of futility. Whoever is in a hurry, shows that the thing he is about, is to big for him. Haste and hurry are very different things.

COMPANY.

To keep good company, especially at our first setting out, is the way to receive good impressions. Good company is not what respective sets of company are pleased either to call or think themselves. It consists chiefly, though not wholly, of people of considerable birth, rank, and character: for people of neither birth nor rank are frequently and very justly admitted into it, if distinguished by any particular merit or eminency in any liberal art or science. So motley a thing is good company, that many people, without birth, rank, or merit, intrude into it by their own forwardness, and others get into it by the protection of some considerable person. In this fashionable good company, the best manners and the purest language are most unquestionably to be learned; for they establish and give the *ton* to both, which are called the language and manners of good company, neither of them being ascertained by any legal tribunal.

A company of people of the first quality cannot be called good company, in the common acceptance of the term, unless they are the fashionable and accredited company of the place; for people of the first quality can be as silly, as ill-bred, and as worthless, as people of the meanest degree. And a company, consisting wholly of people of very low condition, whatever their talents or merit may be, can never be called good company, and therefore should not be much frequented, though by no means despised.

A company wholly composed of learned men, though greatly to be respected, is not meant by the words *Good Company*. They cannot have the easy and polished manners of the world, as they do not live in it. If we can bear our parts well in such a company, it will be proper to be in it sometimes, and we shall be more esteemed in other companies for having a place in that.

A company consisting wholly of professed wits and poets, is very inviting to young men, who are pleased with it, if they have wit themselves; and if they have none, are foolishly proud of being one of it. But such companies should be frequented with moderation and judgment. A wit is a very unpopular denomination, as it carries terror along with it; and people are as much afraid of a wit in company, as a woman is of a gun, which she supposes may go off of itself and do her a mischief. Their acquaintance, however, is worth seeking, and their company worth frequenting; but not to the exclusion of others, nor to such a degree as to be considered only as one of their particular set.

Above all things, endeavour to keep company with people above you, for there you rise as much as you sink with people below. When we say company above you, we do not mean with regard to their birth, but with regard to their merit, and the light in which the world considers them. There are two sorts of good company: one which is called the *beau monde,* and consists of those people who take the lead in the gay part of life. The other consists of those who are distinguished by some particular merit, or who excel in some particular and valuable art or science. Be equally careful to avoid that low company, which in every sense of the word, is low indeed: low in rank, low in parts, and low in manners. Vanity, that source of many of our follies, and of some of our crimes, has sunk many a man into company, in every light infinitely below him, for the sake of being the first man in it. There he dictates, is applauded, and admired; but he soon disgraces himself, and is consequently disqualified for any better company.

INTRODUCTIONS.

Having now spoken of company and the proper behaviour to be observed by all who would wish to be esteemed and respected while mixing much in society, we shall, under this head, consider some of those established rules which relate to introducing one person to another. It is of the greatest importance to know the character and position of the party to whom you wish to be introduced: consequently, you would do well to refuse all offers of introduction except from those in whom you can place the most implicit confidence. How often are regrets expressed when this caution has not been observed. Many a young man has sincerely regretted the time when he was introduced into a circle of acquaintance that he would much rather never have known, when, by a little timely caution on his part, these regrets might never have disturbed him. And since this much is to be said about gentlemen being introduced to society, what shall we say concerning the ladies ?   Truly, the utmost care is necessary, for ladies have not the same means of freeing themselves from an acquaintance with whom they do not wish to be connected, that gentlemen have.   It is extremely disrespectful to any lady to introduce any one to her without having previously acquainted her with your intention. Should she desire you to make the introduction, all is safe and proper.

In the event of your being solicited to give a letter of introduction to a third party, consider the whole circumstances well before proceeding a single step.   If you do not think it consistent with your duty either in respect to the person who asks you for the letter of introduction, or the one to whom it will be addressed, refuse the request firmly, but politely.   It is better to preserve the friendship of one party, than run the risk of losing both by imprudently introducing the one to the other.   In real friendship, to grant an introduction to persons every way suitable, is no less a pleasure than a duty.

Should any one wait upon you with a letter of introduction, politely request the bearer to sit down while you read it.   If you can place implicit confidence in your friend, the writer of the letter, by all means further his wishes in respect to the person who now waits upon you. It is in this way that many warm friendships take their rise, and that many young men going to new situations in new towns, are taken by the hand and preserved, it may be, from companions of a questionable character. It is not usual for ladies to present their letters of introduction personally; the letter should be sent, in all possible circumstances, to the party to whom it is addressed previous to being waited upon.

In travelling, it frequently happens that one person introduces himself to another. Should the stranger conduct himself in a proper and respectful manner, this introduction might turn out to the advantage of both parties; the tedium of the journey might be relieved; objects of interest pointed out &c. All acquaintanceship thus formed, however, should cease at the termination of the journey—as far as ladies are concerned at least.

On a first introduction, it is not customary to shake hands; both parties bow to each other only. It is not until some intimacy has arisen that shaking hands is practised either at meeting or parting. Whatever the difference of rank may be in parties of opposite sexes, the gentleman is always introduced to the lady: and the usual form among gentlemen is that one of an inferior rank is introduced to another of superior, unless there be some exception, such as age or distinction from extrardinary talent or merit.

VISITING AND RECEIVING COMPANY.

Perhaps with the exception of dining, there is not a more important occasion for attention to Etiquette than in the ceremony of visiting. Visits are the medium of much pleasure, and form important threads in those ties which bind us to our relations and friends. We must ever remember that we should weep with those who weep, and rejoice with those who rejoice. Let us mourn with the mourners, and pipe to those who dance. A bow and a visit must always be returned; and no man, however vain, can free himself from this debt which is due to politeness.

There are two kinds of visits: friendly and special. The first of these are generally paid in the morning, or before dinner; very intimate friends visit each other in the evenings. No visit should be made at any inopportune hour, such as breakfast, luncheon, dinner &c., unless specially requested. Should you, however, happen to receive a visit on any of these occasions, show no ill-humour, but make an honest excuse for not attending to your visitor at the time he may be announced. It is not necessary that the lady of the house, in receiving morning visitors, should lay aside any light employment in which she may be engaged, such as needle-work; but it would be extremely impolite not to desist from music, drawing or any other occupation which would completely engross her attention. Visitors should always be received with cordiality, and made thoroughly welcome. Should the visitor be a gentleman, the master of the family, or any in the house at the time, ought to rise on his entrance; if a lady, both ladies and gentlemen should rise. If the visitor approaches to salute a lady, the salute should be acknowledged by the lady half raising herself and slightly bowing.

The whole art of visiting lies in knowing when to leave. It was one of Pelham's maxims always to retire when he had created some sensation in company, because, as he wisely remarks, people are sure to speak well of you, and receive you ever afterwards with unfeigned cordiality. Visits of ceremony should never be long—quarter of an hour is long enough. If you observe the master or mistress of the house look uneasily at the clock, stir the fire frequently, twirl their thumbs, answer your observations in brief sentences, do not hesitate to rise and take your leave at once: where there is any doubt, it is much better to express regret at your departure than impatience at your stay.

In a special visit, let your conversation be confined to the subject which has occasioned it. If it is to congratulate, do it with your best grace; and if it is to condole, strive to alleviate the burden of grief which has fallen upon your friend. There can be no hypocrisy in this; it is the true mission of friendship, and he is poor indeed in heart, who cannot succeed in proving it.

All visits ought to be repaid at the earliest possible convenience, unless there is a great disproportion in rank. Ladies, in paying morning visits, should always do so in *demi-toilette*, that is to say, not in full dress. Such is only reserved for evening parties. A gay and brilliant dress is for the ball alone.

DINING.

Dining is a most important affair in every country. Civilized man talks over his projects, schemes, travels, adventures and what not at the dinner-table. Savages arrange their articles of peace or war over their festive board. There are few events in social life, or perhaps none at all, which occasion such a list of Etiquette requirements to be attended to as this same Dining. When you resolve upon entertaining your friends to dinner, be sure to select those whom you think will prove agreeable to each other. Issue your invitations two or three days beforehand. Those invited should reply immediately, stating whether they accept or decline the invitation. Particular note should be made of the hour at which dinner is to be served; to arrive late is unpardonable. The whole house is disturbed from the master to the cook—to say nothing of the spoilt dinner and the angry guests. Punctuality cannot be too much insisted upon as a virtue in every line of life and on every occasion; but of all occasions which require punctuality, that of dinner is surely one of the very chief. It is only the very great and the very vulgar who make themselves to be waited upon. Some dinner-guests purposely go late in order that they may make a sensation when they enter. Hear what Boileau says on this point:—" I have always been punctual to the hour of dinner, for I knew that those whom I kept waiting, would employ those unpleasant moments to sum up all my faults."

When the announcement is made that dinner is served, do not rush to the dining-room: remain until the master or mistress of the house gives the signal to enter. Offer your left arm to a lady, and conduct her to the diningroom: in doing so, you pass before her, she following without quitting your arm. It may be remarked here that, to pass before a lady in any other circumstance whatever, is a direct breach of Etiquette and good-manners. In the event of there being no ladies present, do not seek to enter the dining-room first; rather, on the contrary, allow every one else to precede you—especially if the guests be your superiors in rank. It is usual for the mistress of the house to take the proffered arm of the guest of greatest distinction, and leading the way, desires him to seat himself beside her. The rest of the guests seat themselves as can most conveniently be done, ladies and gentlemen intermixed as well as possible, not however until the master of the house has given the signal by seating himself. In public dinners, the most distinguished persons present are placed on the right and left of *the chair*, but in private dinner parties, it is found sometimes, that such an arrangement cannot very well be carried out. In whatever position you may be in, attend carefully to the wants and wishes of the ladies beside you, handing them anything most suitable to their tastes, and asking them what more you can do to oblige them. Fairly seated at table, do not show your bad manners by balancing yourself upon your chair, making a tambourine of the table, or stretching your legs under it to annoy, perhaps, your opposite neighbour. If the conversation be general, speak so as to let all hear you if you have anything to say; but if confined to your immediate neighbour, let not your conversation be so loud as to interfere with that of those a little removed from you. If the soup be too hot, dont attempt to cool it by blowing; carry it to your mouth by the side of the spoon.

Never speak with your mouth full; eat slowly, and convey the bread to your mouth in small pieces broken by your fingers only. Fish is eaten with a fork, which should be of silver, as the vinegar is apt to impart to the fish a disagreeable flavour if a steel fork is used. Guests at a dinner-table should never be *pressed*; particular dishes may, however, be recommended. Never lift meat to your mouth with a knife; if a fork be found insufficient use a spoon in preference. At dessert, do not take fruit with a common knife. Do not refuse wine if offered, unless your principles prevent you accepting it—you do not require to do more than taste it.

The mistress of the house gives the signal to rise from the table. The gentlemen, as before, offer their arm to the ladies, and wait upon them to the door. They re-seat themselves at table for wine, after which they join the ladies in the drawing-room.

For subjects of conversation during and after dinner, the reader is referred to the companion volume of this little Manual, "How to Shine in Society," where he will find a full exposition given of the rules relating to this subject.

DANCING.

Ease and grace are to be carefully studied in dancing. The motions of the arms should be particularly attended to, as they decide a man's being genteel or otherwise, more than any other part of the body. A twist or stiffness in the wrist, will make any man look awkward. If a man dances well from the waist upwards, wears his hat well, and moves his head properly, he dances well. Coming into a room, and presenting yourself to a company, should be also attended to, as this always gives the first impression, which is generally the strongest. Those who present themselves well, have a certain dignity in their air, which, without the least seeming mixture of pride, at once engages and is respected. Having stated these general remarks, let us now speak of

THE BALL-ROOM

Where they should be practically carried out. For a Ball or Concert, invitations should be issued at least a week beforehand, in order to give the ladies time to arrange and prepare their dresses. The master of the house, meanwhile, should be arranging matters so that all the ladies who are invited may have an opportunity of dancing. A ball is badly arranged when some of the ladies are never asked to dance, but remain as mere ornaments to the room. In a private dancing party, elderly ladies and gentlemen may with all propriety take part in the different figures, but in a public ball-room, they would do well to refrain and leave the mazy whirls to be performed by younger parties.

Unless you know the figures of a quadrille or any other dance well, you should never rise to take part in them, as you would be sure to produce disorder. Should you, however, be called upon to take part in any dance where you know, probably, the figures only slightly, place yourself in a position where you will not be the first to advance. Attentively observe the movements of those who precede you, and you will soon recollect them enough to get through them creditably.

Preserve the strictest decorum while dancing, and talk little to your partner while so engaged. Do nothing to make yourself vulgar or occasion remark. Lead your partner to a seat at the end of the dance, and thank her for the honour which she has conferred upon you. A gentleman should not manifest undue partiality for any particular partner during the evening, but should distribute his attentions as much as possible. No lady can refuse the invitation of a gentle-man to dance, unless she be previously "engaged." No engagements should be made for more than two dances in advance: three may be permitted, but it is not advisable to do so. Neither married nor young ladies ought to present themselves at a ball without being accompanied by some friend: husband, father, mother, or other attendant. In dancing, however, such relations should never be used as partners. No one should appear without white gloves at any dancing party, either public or private.

It is customary for gentlemen to offer their partner refreshments at public balls. The lady, however, is quite at liberty to accept or not accept this attention; unless she is intimately acquainted with him who prof-fers this kindness, it would be well to act with caution. In private dancing-parties, every one is free to accept the refreshments provided by the host or hostess.

No one should remain at a ball longer than they feel disposed; it is better to leave at once when one feels inclined to do so than remain, and be the worse for it next day. Use due moderation in this as in many other things, and the evening's amusement will always bear the morning's reflection. Take your leave in a way that will disturb neither the mistress of the house nor any of her guests; and should you have enjoyed yourself during the evening, take an early opportunity of calling upon your entertainers and thank them for the pleasure you experienced.

THE CONCERT.

Concerts are either public or private, and the rules of Etiquette to be observed on such occasions differ accordingly. The one half of people who attend them go for the sake of being seen; the other half go to hear the entertainment provided in the article of music. Should it be an amateur concert, it is exceedingly probable you may find the audience caring more for seeing than hearing; but if a professional one, the greatest attention ought to be paid to the singing or instrumental music. Should you feel pleased and gratified dont applaud voiciferously, if you do applaud at all: rather maintain a profound silence. It is exceedingly vulgar to annoy your neighbours by beating time, humming the tunes, or making unseemly and ridiculous gestures of admiration. Should you unfortunately not feel interested in the performance, endeavour to conceal your disappointment as philosophically as possible. There may be people beside you, who are charmed and delighted: your uneasy attitudes and wry faces might spoil their whole enjoyment. Think of their feelings toward you: would they be friendly, or the reverse?

AMUSEMENTS.

Every period of life has amusements which are natural and proper to it. You may indulge the variety of your tastes in these, while you keep within the bounds of that propriety which is suitable to either sex. Some amusements are conducive to health, as various kinds of exercise. Some are connected with qualities really useful; as different kinds of women's work, and all the domestic concerns of a family. Some are elegant accomplishments, as dress, dancing, music, and drawing. Such books as improve the understanding, enlarge the circle of knowledge, and cultivate good taste, may be considered in a higher point of view than mere amusements; there are a variety of others, which are neither useful nor ornamental: such as plays of different kinds.

There are four words in our language used to denote

the stepping aside, as it were, for a little while from the occupations of life to enjoy a change. These are relaxation, diversion, amusement, and recreation. The idea of the first of these is taken from a bow which, in order to keep up its spring and elasticity, must be unbent when not required for use. A person cannot always be at work: he must unbend the bow to keep himself fresh and ready for it after some relaxation. Diversion signifies a turning aside from the pursuits of this life to see something curious or uncommon; amusement means the laying apart for a while the study of the muses; and by recreation we understand the refreshing of the mental faculties when they are overtasked or burdened by care or anxiety. From all these considerations, then, we infer that we were not sent into this world to idle away our time, but to be up and doing something. The bow is not kept to be always unbent, so if we make relaxation the business of life, its nature is totally changed. The bed is sweet to a tired and weary man, but it soon becomes anything but refreshing when he is confined to it longer than usual. The sentence to the effect that he who does not work shall not eat, applies equally to the rich man and to the poor one. If the former does not employ himself in some way or other to benefit the public, he scarcely ever fails to become a burden to himself and a prey to *ennui*. To be useful is to be happy. A blessing accompanies every useful employment; it keeps a man on good terms with himself, and gives him a capacity of being pleased with every innocent gratification. The mind and the body are intimately connected; and just as labour is necessary to procure an appetite to the former, so the latter must have some previous exercise to prepare it for enjoyment. Happiness is after all, pretty equally distributed, when we compare the different lots of mankind. The industrious poor have, in many respects, more real enjoyment of life than the idle and dissolute of the wealthier classes, who, by their abuse of wealth and power, and their immoderate pursuit of imaginary pleasures fall into temptations and snares. The end of these things is death.

All exercise which obliges us to be much in the open air is highly commendable. Attention to health is a duty we owe to ourselves and to our friends. Bad health seldom fails to have an influence on the spirits and temper. The finest geniuses, the most delicate minds, have very frequently a corresponding delicacy of bodily constitution, which they are too apt to neglect. A gentleman should always attend even to the *choice* of his amusements. "Music," says Lord Chesterfield in his famous letters to his son on men and manners, "Music is usually reckoned one of the liberal arts, and not unjustly; but a man of fashion who is seen piping or fiddling at a concert, degrades his own dignity. If you love music hear it; pay fiddlers to play to you, but never fiddle yourself. It makes a gentleman appear frivolous and contemptible, leads him frequently into bad company, and wastes that time which might otherwise be well employed." Now, although, we can scarcely indorse the whole of these sentiments, yet we give his Lordship full credit for the valuable lesson which he wishes to teach his son. Choose your amusements, and let them be such as will tend in every way to improve your understanding, enlarge your knowledge, and cultivate your taste.

LETTER-WRITING.

Letter-writing, if we may judge from the estimation in which it was held by the Romans, seems to have formed a part of their regular education, and to have been considered as a liberal and polite accomplishment. The epistles of Cicero are regarded as among the most perfect models of writing. In the opinion of Locke, this useful and important art well deserves the same attention from ourselves. " The writing of letters," he observes, " enters so much into all the occasions of life, that no gentleman can avoid showing himself in compositions of this kind. Occurrences will daily force him to make this use of his pen, which lays open his breeding, his sense and his abilities, to a severer examination than any oral discourse." With the exception of Cowper, Cowley, Gay and a few more, our language can boast of very few writers who may be regarded as models of letter-writing. If we pass to other nations we find that Cicero's epistles to Atticus, and to his intimate friends, are the best examples in the friendly and familiar style. The simplicity and clearness of the letters of Cardinal d'Ossat show how letters of business ought to be written. For gay and amusing letters, there are none that equal Compte Bussy's and Madame Sevigne's. They are so natural that they seem to be the extempore conversation of two people of wit, rather than letters.

Letters should be easy and natural, and convey to the persons to whom we send them, just what we would say to those persons if we were present with them. The chief property of style in epistolary composition is simply a good choice of words, properly constructed and clearly expressed. " I would have my letters," says Seneca, " to be like my discourses, when we either sit or walk together, unstudied and easy." But as the subjects of letters are so exceedingly varied, so ought they to have considerable variety in the manner of expression. If you are narrating any circumstance to your friend, do it clearly and distinctly; if preferring a request, do it modestly; if exhorting, write in a lively and vigorous manner, and if consoling, be kind and compassionate. There is another matter to be considered, which also requires a difference in the modes of expression; namely, the character and position of the person to whom we address our communication. Superiors are to be addressed respectfully, inferiors courteously, and equals civilly. But when friends and acquaintances write to each other, they ought to adapt their style so as to resemble as much as possible their ordinary conversation; because, when parted, they cannot enjoy each other's society, so the next best thing in the circumstances, is to converse by letters. Hence, the more natural your method of communication is, the more will your friend enjoy your letter. Cicero says, "a letter does not blush," in allusion to the fact that sometimes greater freedom is used in epistles than the same persons would have taken in conversing with each other; but it is well to guard against saying anything in a letter which would not be suitable for ordinary discourse.

A person who can write letters anonymously or under an assumed name, for the purpose of vilifying any one's good name, is one upon whom all good advice is lost. If you receive any injury, verbally, or in writing, reply if possible; but if circumstances compel you to reply in writing, do so firmly but politely.

All letter-writers ought to have a subject whereon to write; there should at least be one leading idea, and, if so disposed, a correspondent can fill up the remainder of his space, if he has any, with anything that he considers might amuse or interest his friend. In letters of business, there is no supplementary matter to the main subject. In corresponding with friends, never employ an amanuensis or secretary, and never write upon blank leaves torn from some other person's notes to you. Let your paper be good; to write on very coarse paper is allowed only to the most indigent; to se gilt-edged and highly perfumed for letters of business would be simply ridiculous. The date of a letter is one of its most important points: it is frequently necessary to the right understanding of its contents, therefore never omit the date. Write it at the right hand corner on the first page of your paper.

No letter should be allowed to lie long unanswered; it is an impoliteness to the writer of it. This observation applies to business letters in particular: neatness in folding up and directing a letter is by no means to be neglected.   There is something in the exterior of a letter, that may please or displease, and consequently, it deserves some attention.

Our space forbids us to give precise directions regarding the forms of address.   A letter to a business firm where two or more are in partnership is addressed, at the beginning of the communication, by the term " Gentlemen," while " Sir," is used to one person, or to an individual with whom we are but slightly acquainted.   " Dear Sir," or " My Dear Sir," are used to express the different degrees of intimacy. The form " I have the honour to be, Gentlemen, (or Sir), your most obedient Servant," is that usually employed in concluding a letter. We dare not here venture—there are actually some books that do—to give any hint regarding lovers' letters.   That is too sacred a subject for a Manual of Etiquette to meddle with.

DRESS AND THE TOILETTE.

Dress is one of the various ingredients that contribute to the art of pleasing, and therefore an object of some attention ; for we cannot help forming some opinions of a man's sense and character from his dress. All affectation in dress implies a flaw in the understanding. Men of sense carefully avoid any particular character in their dress; they are accordingly clean for their own sake, but all the rest is for the sake of other people. A man should dress as well, and in the same manner, as the people of sense and fashion of the place where he is: if he dresses more than they, he is a fop: if he dresses less, he is unpardonably negligent. Of the two, a young man should be rather too much than too little dressed; the excess of that side will wear off with a little age and reflection. Before marriage, he ought to follow the fashion in so far as it is not ridiculous; after that event in his life, he should continue to do the same thing, but in a more modified degree. Both young, and other gentlemen ought, in every case, to conform to that mode which is fashionable in the best society.

The same remarks apply to ladies. Neatness and plainness are, after all, what go to form a well dressed lady. Not so much plainness either, for that would be set down by some people to the account of meanness, just in the same way as the opposite extreme would be charged to that of extravagance. Dress expresses character, consequently, vanity, or slovenliness will at once be exhibited by the kind of attire.

Avoid a profusion of rings, chains, jewellery, &c., and even keep in mind that a lady moving in good society ought to be characterised, in regard to her dress, by good taste and simplicity, not however, to the exclusion of elegance. Should your taste in the choice of colour, selection of patterns, or the external arrangement of your dress, not be good, ask some friend so gifted to assist you. In every case adapt your dress and toilette to your age, and also to the particular time of the day and season of the year. In the morning, they should be simple and neat: the same when making morning visits, and for the evening, they should be richer and more elegant. In summer, wear light thin garments of delicate colours, and in winter, thick and warm clothing. Ladies should remember too, that particular attention is necessary in choosing a dress, to see that the pattern will conform to her stature, and the colour to her complexion. If of short dimensions, a large pattern and deep trimmings will dwarf them still more; and every thing should be avoided that would give undue prominence to any personal defect or peculiarity, as, for instance, a warm, fresh complexion would be made to appear still warmer were a bonnet worn lined with red, or having much ribbon about it of the same colour.

Young unmarried ladies are not allowed to wear such rich and costly dresses as married ones, whatever their fortune or prospects may be. Married ladies, on the other hand, should keep in mind that a good, simple taste in dress, will save much domestic discomfort that invariably arises from extravagance in dress. Gloves, trifling as they may appear, give the finishing touch to a lady's dress. They should invariably be worn when out of doors, whether visiting, shopping, at church, concerts, or any place of amusement or public resort. White gloves are worn only in full dress; the colour of the dress should regulate the hues of those worn on other occasions. Flowers are most suitable for balls, evening parties, and other assemblies.

A few more words to the gentlemen on the subject of dress, before proceeding to the toilette. In whatever style you wear your coat, let it, as well as the rest of your dress be of good material and well made; and when you find a clothier to your mind, keep by him and he will endeavour to suit you to the best of his ability. Morning visits or those not of a ceremonious nature, are generally made in a frock or other coat, good black hat, coloured tie and gloves. The full-dress of a gentleman consists of the black cloth vest, trousers of the same material and colour, black patent leather boots, black silk tie and whit-

cravat. "Got up" in such a costume, a gentleman may appear, with acceptance, at any dinner table, evening party, ball, theatre, or opera.

Cleanliness is the first requisite of the toilette. In these days in which we live, no one can find any excuse for neglecting personal cleanliness. Baths of every description are within the reach of all; to descant upon their merits here would be totally out of place. Cleanliness is next to godliness. The hair and nails should be carefully attended to; the latter should be cut once a-week and brushed clean every morning. The teeth require perhaps more care than any of these; if we would wish to keep them free from decay's approach, the mouth should be washed out after every meal. If the knife wherewith we cut our food at table requires to be cleaned after every time it has been used, why should we not take the same trouble with our teeth? Why indeed? Soft tooth-brushes are recommended in preference to hard ones, and be careful what kind of tooth-powder is employed. Use perfumes sparingly, and *face powder* never! With which sage advice, gentle reader, we close these remarks and pass on to another subject.

ETIQUETTE OF THE STREET.

Were the following simple rule always reduced to practice when walking on the street, " keep to the right," it would prevent that unseemidly jostling which is so often witnessed in our crowded thoroughfares. One stream of passengers keeping their " right," would pass those coming in the opposite direction without the slightest inconvenience. In overtaking passengers going in the same direction as yourself, pass them on whichever side you can most conveniently do so. Endeavour in any case, always to cause the least trouble in meeting or passing any lady, old or infirm persons, and persons of superior rank. If you have a lady on your arm, give her the side next the wall or houses, as you will thereby prevent her from being inconvenienced by the other passengers. Should a carriage, passing, stop the current of people for a few minutes, dont get impatient; it cant be helped; others are in exactly the same predicament. If the weather be wet or damp, take care not to splash with mud any one you pass. No lady ought to raise her dress higher than the ancle, and in supporting it, she should use the right hand only. Umbrellas ought to be carried so as, when up, they will cause no inconvenience to the other passengers on the street. Should a lady be overtaken in a shower, and be unprovided with an umbrella she ought to be careful how she accepts the offer of one from a gentleman; in most cases, she would do well to refuse it with politeness, and take shelter in some shop or doorway, but if pressed for time and she have an engagement to be fulfilled, the offer may be accepted with all propriety. It is extremely rude, and shows an utter want of good-breeding to stoop down and stare a lady in the face while in the street. A gentleman who could do such an act of impoliteness, not to speak of impropriety, does not deserve the name of one.

It is not necessary that you should stop to speak to any one on the street whom you may happen to know. Possibly his time, or your own, may not allow of such being done. You may judge from his manner of walking whether or not he is inclined to speak; if he pass you hurriedly, do not detain him. In the event of your meeting a person whom you may wish to consult on matters of business or otherwise, instead of detaining him, walk in the direction in which he is going. Should he, on the contrary, wish to consult you, he ought to consider your time, and accompany you.

If you meet a lady, bow respectfully, lifting your hat at the same time, but, unless the acquaintance is one of long standing, she, according to the rules of etiquette, bows first. Remember this too, that a gentleman should never stop a lady on the street, unless he has got something to communicate to her.

It is very improper to speak to any one on the street from a window, or to make any signs to passengers below. Gentlemen need not be reminded also, that it is a breach of manners to smoke in the streets.

THE PROMENADE.

Assume no majestic or ridiculous airs on the public promenade, and do not sing or talk in a loud or vulgar manner. The strictest decorum, indeed, ought to be observed by all who would wish themselves to be respected. When you give your arm to a lady, Etiquette does not exact from you that you should carry her shawl, parasol, &c.; but if you have any gallantry about you, you will do so. Regulate your pace to that of hers, and do not walk too fast. Pick your footsteps. It is extremely vulgar for a lady to take the arms of two gentlemen. Should there be more ladies in the party than gentlemen, the latter ought to offer their arm to the eldest lady, or to the most exalted in rank, in preference to all the others. Gentlemen may conduct two ladies at the same time, one in each arm, if occasion requires; but this is seldom done. If there are seats on the promenade, no lady should sit down without some one of her party beside her—a husband, son, daughter, companion, or attendant: it would be an impropriety to do so. In walking with two persons of superior rank to yourself, do not walk between them, but on their left.

To gentlemen is reserved the honour of paying for everything in the way of expense incurred at places of public promenade, such as carriages, bouquets at the gardens, or sweetmeats for the children (if any.) Never walk in advance of any one who accompanies you on a promenade. If you wish to look at any object, ask your companion to stop and do the same.

Should you be on horseback in company with a lady, do not mount your horse before she does so; always see that she is mounted first, and when she is in the saddle properly, hand her the riding whip. Allow the lady to regulate the pace of the horse. Ride by her right side, but do not let the head of your horse advance beyond the shoulders of hers, unless she desires you. Should the weather be windy, or the roads dusty, quit the right side if necessary, and take that position that will best shelter her. Be constantly ready to attend upon your fair companion, and keep a careful look-out in case of anything going wrong with the harness of her horse.

If you are riding with a gentleman who is your
superior, allow him to mount first, and should there be
no other person to hold his horse while he does so, do
it yourself. The place of honour is on the right side;
but if more than yourself accompany a man of rank,
allow those next to him in rank to ride by his side.

AT HOME IN THE FAMILY.

Every master of a house should be able to acquit
himself creditably before company in the following
matters, which, trifling as they may appear, yet must be
done by all who desire to feel at ease in whatever position they may be placed. He should, first of all, be
able to do the honours of the table gracefully. Carving
is a small matter, apparently; yet how uncomfortable
he must feel who cannot dissect a fowl or cut up a roast
without hacking away at the bones for a quarter of an
hour, and bespattering every body near him with grease
or sauce. A little attention to this necessary art as
opportunity daily presents itself, is all that is necessary
to become proficient in this graceful accomplishment.

Perhaps of all matters that cause most anxiety to the
mistress of the house, in connection with domestic

arrangements, is that under the head of servants, who too often prove a source of much unpleasantness in families.   There are, indeed, some striking exceptions of servants who consider the interests of their master and mistress as their own, and who endeavour by all means in their power to serve them well.   But how many are there, on the other hand, who but too frequently prove domestic enemies, whose views, designs, and inclinations are altogether opposed to those of their mistress !   Whatever character they bear, or whatever behaviour they manifest, no lady should trust them too much nor treat them with undue familiarity.   But this does not affect in any degree that spirit of kindness with which every mistress should show towards her servants on every possible occasion.   When reproof is necessary, that reproof should be conveyed calmly, but firmly, and never in presence of company.   The mistress of a house should train her servants to habits of obedience, economy, civility and politeness.   They ought never to be allowed to appear before company either too carelessly or too gaudily dressed, and when spoken to, should be addressed by their christian name, or if there are many in the house, by the names of their duties, such as nurse, housemaid, &c.   Mistresses will do well to rule with leniency, and rather exceed their contract with their servants, than make the least abatement.   A little concession to them is a great boon, and as we would advise mistresses to see that the household duties are properly carried out, both as regards manner and time, so we would also recommend them to indulge their servants with an occasional holiday or certain hours of recreation, now and again: it keeps them in temper, health, and spirits, and is really their right, in equity, though the favour be granted from policy.

ECONOMY.

Economy is so important a part of woman's education, so necessary to her own happiness, and so essential to her performing properly the duties of a wife and of a mother, that it ought to have the precedence of all other accomplishments, and take its rank next to the first duties of life. It is moreover an *art* as well as a virtue, and many well-meaning persons, either from ignorance or from want of thought, are strangely deficient in it. Indeed, it is too often wholly neglected in a young woman's education, and she is sent from her father's house to govern a family, without the least degree of that knowledge which should qualify her for it. This is the source of much inconvenience, for though experience and attention may supply, by degrees, the want of instruction, yet this requires time; the family in the meantime may get into habits which are very difficult to alter, and what is worse, the husband's opinion of his wife's incapacity may be fixed too strongly to suffer him ever to think justly of her gradual improvement.

Economy consists of so many branches that it is only possible here to give a mere outline of them. The first and greatest point is to lay out your general plan of living in a just proportion to your income and position in society. If these two will not coincide, the latter must certainly give way; for, if you have right principles, you cannot fail of being wretched under the sense of the injustice as well as danger of spending beyond your income, and your distress will be continually increasing. No mortifications, which you can suffer from retrenching in your appearance, can be comparable to this unhappiness. Regularity of payments and accounts is essential to economy. Housekeeping bills should be settled at least once a week; all other tradesmen should be paid at regularly stated intervals. You must endeavour to acquire skill in purchasing. In order to do this, you should begin to attend to the prices of things, and take every proper opportunity of learning the real value of everything, as well as the marks whereby you are to distinguish the good from the bad. In your table, as in your dress, and in all other things, aim at propriety and neatness, or if your state demands it, elegance, rather than superfluous figure. The neatness and order of your house and furniture is a part of economy which will greatly affect your character and appearance, and to which you must yourself give attention, since it is not possible even for the *rich* and *great* to rely wholly on the care of servants, in such points, without their being often neglected. The more magnificently a house is furnished, the more one is disgusted with the air of confusion which often prevails where attention is wanting in the owner; but on the other hand, there is a kind of neatness, which gives a lady the air of a house-maid, and makes her excessively troublesome to everybody, and particularly to her husband. In this, as in all other branches of economy, avoid all parade and bustle.

Domestic economy, and the credit and happiness of a family, depend so much on the choice and proper regulation of servants, that it must be considered an essential part both of prudence and duty. But we need not pursue these remarks farther, as we have clearly touched on the topics of servants already. Let us only say, in conclusion, that the study of economy, and a rational plan of expense, will save the mistress of the house from many corroding cares, and at the same time give her the full and liberal enjoyment of what she does spend.

FRIENDSHIP.

There is a good difference between the terms, friend and companion; it is a great mistake to suppose they have the same meaning. Many people have companions, but how few really have true friends! A very complaisant and agreeable companion may, and often does, prove a very improper and a very dangerous friend. People will, in a great degree, form their opinion of you upon that which they have of your friends; and there is a Spanish proverb which says, very justly " Tell-me whom you live with, and I will tell you what you are." One may fairly suppose that a man, who makes a knave or a fool his friend, has something very bad to do, or to conceal. But, at the same time that you carefully decline the friendship of knaves and fools, if it can be called friendship, there is no occasion to make either of them your enemies, wantonly and unprovoked, for they are a numerous class, and it is better to choose a secure neutrality, than alliance or war with either of them. You may be a declared enemy to their vices and follies, without being marked out by them as a personal one. Their enmity is the next dangerous thing to their friendship. Have a real reserve with almost every body; and have a seeming reserve with almost nobody; for it is very disagreeable to seem reserved, and very dangerous not to be so. Few people find the true medium; many are ridiculously mysterious and reserved upon trifles, and many imprudently communicative of all they know.

In the choice of your friends, have your principal regard to goodness of heart and fidelity. If they also possess taste and genius, that will still make them more agreeable and useful companions. But you cannot be too wary in your choice, for it is no light matter trusting one's happiness to another person's keeping. Should you find a friend with many amiable qualities, and be thereby induced to cultivate a more than ordinary friendship, do not profess more than you design to perform, and when you oblige let it be done in such a way as to let him feel you really do it from a feeling of respect and attachment towards him. If possible, when doing some service to your friend, spare his modesty, and endeavour to make him feel that you are happy in being able to have this opportunity of reciprocating his sentiments. But in this, as in all other things, you are to be guided very much by discretion. Any interest you can make, time you can devote, or ready money you can spare, for furthering the good estate of your friend, is nobly bestowed; and, if after all, he should prove ungrateful, do not upbraid him

But there is a friendship which young persons especially should be guarded against. With an unguarded frank-

ness about them, young people often become the easy
prey of the artful and experienced. They look upon
every knave or fool, who tells them he is their friend, to
be really so, and pay that simulated friendship with an
indiscreet and unbounded confidence, always to their loss,
often to their ruin. Beware of these proffered friendships.
Receive them with great civility, but with great incredul-
ity too; and pay them with compliments, but not with
confidence. Do not suppose that people become friends
at first sight, or even upon a short acquaintance. Real
friendship is of slow growth; and never thrives unless
ingrafted upon a stock of known and reciprocal merit.

COURTSHIP.

We come now to speak of another kind of friendship,
but one of a very " near and dear" description. And as
we have now arrived at a most important subject—no
less than a very delicate one—let us in the first instance,
say a few words to the fairer portion of our readers.

What is love? To give a proper answer to this mo-
mentous question is, we conceive, next to impossible. If
we get excited and warm upon the subject, those of a
quiet and subdued deportment, set us down as enthusi-

asts: if, on the other hand, we speak of it in a calm and collected manner, the ardent lover pooh-poohs the whole affair. No, all things considered, we would rather leave the solution of the question to each individual; this, we consider, will be by far the most satisfactory way.

If there is any secret that cannot be disclosed even to a friend, that secret must surely be "a love affair." Though a woman has no reason to be ashamed of her attachment to a man of merit, yet nature, whose authority is superior to philosophy, has annexed a sense of shame to it. It is even long before a woman of delicacy dares avow to her own heart that she loves; and, when all the subterfuges of ingenuity to conceal it from herself fail, she feels a violence done both to her pride, and to her modesty. This is especially the case when she is not sure of a return to her attachment. Of all the secrets that are worst kept, love affairs rank first; because a woman who confides them to her friend generally discovers that however important she herself may regard them, that friend often considers them as trifling, and subjects of pleasantry more than anything else. If, therefore, you must have a friend to pour out your heart to, be sure of her honour and secrecy.

It is a maxim laid down among ladies, and a very prudent one it is, that love is not to begin on their part, but is entirely to be the consequence of men's attach-

ment to them.   As, therefore, nature has not given you
that unlimited range in your choice which men enjoy,
she has wisely and benevolently assigned to you a greater
flexibility of taste on this subject.   Some agreeable
qualites recommend a gentleman to your common good
liking and friendship.   In the course of his acquaintance
he contracts an attachment to you.   When you perceive
it, it excites your gratitude; this gratitude rises into
preference; and this preference, perhaps, at last advances
to some degree of attachment, especially if it meets with
crosses and difficulties; for these, and a state of suspense,
are very great incitements to attachment, and are the
food of love in both sexes.   The effects of love among
men are diversified by their different tempers.   A man
of delicacy often betrays his passion by his too great
anxiety to conceal it, especially if he has little hopes of
success.   True love, in all its stages, seeks concealment,
and never expects success; it renders a man not only
respectful, but timid to the highest degree in his behaviour
to the woman he loves.   His heart and his character will
be improved in every respect by his attachment: his
manners will become more gentle, and his conversation
more agreeable; but diffidence and embarrassment will
always make him appear to disadvantage in the presence
of her whom he loves.

When you observe, then, in a gentleman's behaviour
these marks just described, reflect seriously what you
are to do.   If his attachment is agreeable to you, allow
nature, good sense, and delicacy to direct you.   If you
love him, never discover to him the full extent of your
love—no, not although you marry him.   That suffi-

ciently shows your preference, which is all he is entitled to know. If he has delicacy, he will ask for no stronger proof of your affection for *your* sake; if he has sense, he will not ask it for his *own*. On the other hand, if you are determined to shut your heart against him, treat him honourably and humanely; do not let him linger in a miserable suspense, but be anxious to let him know your sentiments with regard to him. You may easily show that you wish to avoid his company; but if he is a man whose friendship you wish to preserve, you may not choose this method, because then you love him in every capacity. You may get a common friend to explain matters to him, or fall on many other devices, if you are seriously anxious to put him out of suspense. If he brings you to an explanation, give him a polite but resolute and decisive answer. In whatever way you convey your sentiments to him, if he is a man of spirit and delicacy, he will give you no further trouble, nor apply to your friends for their interference.

When women endeavour to justify themselves to the world, and to their own conscience, after acting otherwise than in the manner just described and recommended, they have many excuses. They plead either ignorance, or uncertainty of the gentleman's real sentiments : sometimes it is the decorum of their sex, they say, which enjoins an equal behaviour to all men, and forbids them to consider any man as a lover till he has directly told them so. But vanity and the love of admiration are generally at the bottom of this conduct, and it is not till every art of coquetry fails to keep a lover, that a lady is forced to make an explanation. Male coquetry is much more inexcusable than female, as well as more pernicious.   A man of parts, sentiment, and address, laying aside all regard to truth and humanity, may engage the hearts of fifty women at the same time; and may likewise conduct his coquetry with so much art, as to put it out of the power of any of them to specify a single expression that could be said to be directly expressive of love. This ambiguity of behaviour, this art of keeping one in suspense, is the great secret of coquetry in both sexes.   But it is the more cruel in men, because they can carry it what length they please, and as long as they please, without the ladies being so much at liberty as to complain or expostulate; whereas, a gentleman can break the connexion, and force a lady to explain whenever he becomes impatient of the situation.

The gentleman's choice of a wife should be conducted on the following rational principles.   Let her not be of a family who boast of name, connections, or wealth, but of one remarkable, rather, for their simple manners and spotless character.   Let the lady's own character be clear and unimpeachable, and if she have any pride, let it be that proceeding from a feeling of her own innocence.   If you marry a beauty, remember that you may have a thorn in your side thereby: it is not all likely that she will allow you to be to her anything but a mere appendix, and if she rule, which is very probable, she will rule with a high hand.   But do not despise beauty, either; only be sure that that is not the only recommendation she possesses.   If she has much good nature, is a good manager, has a comfortable portion, and no poor relations—why then, so much the better: we envy the happiness in store for you.   He that findeth a good wife really findeth a good thing.

MARRIAGE.

Whatever the views of either sex are in marrying, every possible precaution should be taken to prevent these views being disappointed. If fortune, and the pleasures it brings, are your aim, it is not sufficient that the settlements of a jointure and children's provisions be ample, and properly secured, but it is necessary that you should enjoy the fortune during your own life.   It would be ungenerous to take advantage of a lover's attachment, to plunge him into distress; and if he has any honour, no personal gratification will ever tempt him to enter into any connexion which will render you unhappy.   If you have as much between you as to satisfy all your demands, it is sufficient.

The fact, that though many men marry, yet comparatively few live happily, proves that there is more art necessary to keep affection alive than to procure its gratification.   This is an important matter, and deserves careful consideration.   The married state, if entered into from proper motives of esteem and regard, will be a happy one for both parties, and to the husband we would say, now that you have got the object of your choice secure in possession, do not depreciate or neglect her. How miserable must that woman become when she sees, shortly after entering into such a solemn and enduring union as marriage, that he whom she has taken " for better, for worse," is being gradually transformed from the once servile lover to the tyrant husband. When indifference begins, neglect, contempt, and aversion soon follow. For your own peace, no less than for hers, endeavour at all times to make her feel that she is still as dear to you as ever. Take pleasure in your own home, and do not seek other company in preference to hers; let her really be a companion, the sharer with you in all your pleasures, and give her frequent opportunities of finding out for herself that it is her own fault, if she is not the happiest woman alive.

But unpleasantness may arise, and clouds obscure the fair landscape; for even in the best regulated families, there are times when such things happen. When these do arise, however, make not things worse by giving way to peevishness or anger, bitter expressions or dogged sullenness. Both of you are alike subject to frailties, therefore you may reasonably expect offences too. When they do come, forget and forgive. Love, like charity, should cover a multitude of sins, and, depend upon it, that the more obstinate of the two is the more foolish. As you have been made one by the ties of marriage, so let there be no separate interests in the household; be modest in your style of living, conforming always to the means at your disposal from your income. Entertain company not often; and when you do have some friends, do not swell out the pride of a day to such exhorbitant dimensions, that you will have to curtail your expenses in the family for a month to come. Have ready money to go to market with; for whoso runs in debt for his provisions will soon have a mill-stone about his neck.

In the education of your children, there are three things to be attended to and remembered: first, take care of their health, then their morals; and finally, provide them with such an education as will enable them to make their way successfully in the world. Teach them useful knowledge, and bring them up to learn some business or profession, for that is the surest way to preserve an estate when got. They should ever be taught, too, to remember that the command enjoined in the Sacred Scriptures:—" Honour thy father and thy mother," is one which proceeds from the highest authority. It is the first commandment which has a promise attached as a reward for its due observance.

"The Last Scene of All."

FUNERALS.

Every country, and almost every district has its own particular ceremonies at funerals. Those peculiar to Scotland are admirably depicted by Scott in the " Antiquary " at the burial of Steenie Mucklebackit. The scene is too long to be extracted, and would be spoiled by abridgement, we refer the reader to the book itself.

We may remark generally, under this heading, that ill health or the most important business can only be accepted as an excuse for non-attendance at a funeral to which you have been specially invited. Arrive punctually at the time stated, and let your dress and behaviour be in accordance with the occasion,—grave and silent. If carriages have been provided, allow the relations and intimate friends to take precedence; and if on foot, regulate your distance by the degree of your intimacy. When the body is laid in the grave, reverently uncover your head, and bow adieu.

And now our task is ended. On looking over the pages, it seems " a sorry sight," and perhaps we have not done it either wisely or too well. The majority of mankind however are ignorant, and generally foolish, but are wisely anxious for instruction, therefore is it, that many books are written, are popular, and sell, and so will it be to

THE END.